ebble®

ch It Grow

Milkweed Bugs

by Martha E. H. Rustad
Consulting editor: Gail Saunders-Smith, PhD

Consultant: Laura Jesse
Plant and Insect Diagnostic Clinic
Iowa State University, Ames, Iowa

Capstone
press®

Mankato, Minnesota

Pebble Books are published by Capstone Press,
151 Good Counsel Drive, P.O. Box 669, Mankato, Minnesota 56002.
www.capstonepress.com

1 2 3 4 5 6 14 13 12 11 10 09

Library of Congress Cataloging-in-Publication Data
Rustad, Martha E. H. (Martha Elizabeth Hillman), 1975–
    Milkweed bugs / by Martha E. H. Rustad.
    p. cm. — (Pebble Books. Watch it grow)
    Includes bibliographical references and index.
    Summary: "Simple text and photographs present the life cycle of milkweed
bugs" — Provided by publisher.
        ISBN-13: 978-1-4296-2227-1 (hardcover) ISBN-10: 1-4296-2227-X (hardcover)
        ISBN-13: 978-1-4296-3444-1 (softcover)   ISBN-10: 1-4296-3444-8 (softcover)
1. Large milkweed bug — Juvenile literature. I. Title.
QL523.L9.R87 2009
595.7′54 — dc22   2008026938

Note to Parents and Teachers

The Watch It Grow set supports national science standards related to life science. This book describes and illustrates milkweed bugs. The images support early readers in understanding the text. The repetition of words and phrases helps early readers learn new words. This book also introduces early readers to subject-specific vocabulary words, which are defined in the Glossary section. Early readers may need assistance to read some words and to use the Table of Contents, Glossary, Read More, Internet Sites, and Index sections of the book.

Table of Contents

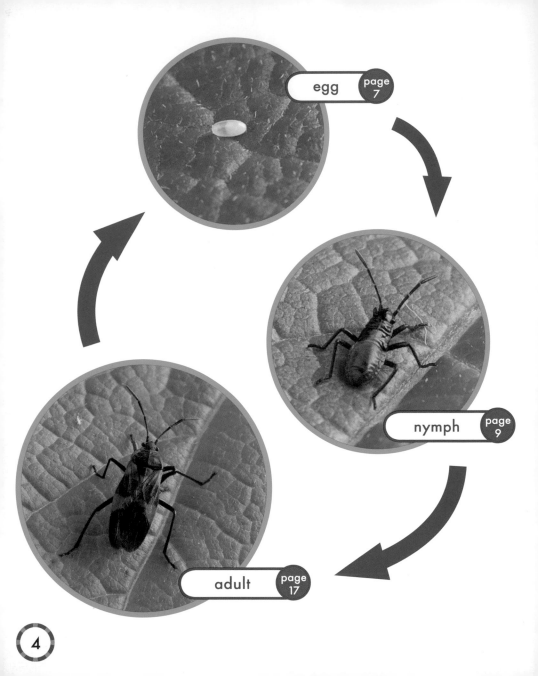

egg page 7

nymph page 9

adult page 17

4

Metamorphosis

Milkweed bugs are orange and black insects. These insects go through metamorphosis as they grow.

egg

From Egg to Nymph

Milkweed bugs
begin life as eggs.
Females lay tiny eggs
on milkweed plants.

8

Over five days, the eggs
turn orange.
Then, nymphs hatch
from the eggs.

Nymphs look much like
adult milkweed bugs.
But unlike adults,
they are mostly orange
and don't have wings.

mouth

Nymphs eat and grow.
They suck juice
from milkweed seed pods
with their tube-shaped mouths.

Nymphs molt as they grow.
They shed their
hard outer shells.
With each molt,
their wings grow larger.

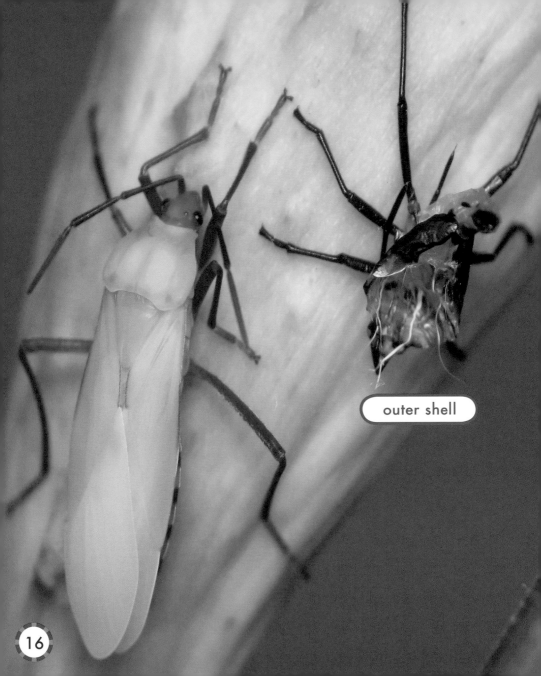

outer shell

From Nymph to Adult

After the fifth molt, milkweed bugs are adults. At first, adults have yellow bodies and orange legs.

In a few hours, adults turn dark orange and black. Adult milkweed bugs have two wings and six legs.

Eating milkweed plants makes milkweed bugs taste bad to predators. Milkweed helps these bugs stay safe.

Glossary

hatch — to break out of an egg

insect — a small animal with a hard outer shell, six legs, three body sections, and two antennae; most insects have wings.

metamorphosis — the series of changes some animals go through as they develop from eggs to adults

molt — to shed an outer shell or layer of skin so a new covering can be seen; when this process happens once, it is also called a molt.

nymph — a young form of an insect; nymphs change into adults by shedding their outer shell many times.

predator — an animal that hunts and eats other animals

Read More

Holland, Mary. *Milkweed Visitors.* Glenshaw, Penn.: Bas Relief Publishing and Monarchs in the Classroom, 2006.

Kalman, Bobbie, and Kelley MacAulay. *Meadow Food Chains.* Food Chains. New York: Crabtree, 2005.

Internet Sites

FactHound offers a safe, fun way to find educator-approved Internet sites related to this book.

Here's what you do:

1. Visit *www.facthound.com*
2. Choose your grade level.
3. Begin your search.

This book's ID number is **9781429622271.**

FactHound will fetch the best sites for you!

Index

Word Count: 144
Grade: 1
Early-Intervention Level: 17

Editorial Credits
Erika L. Shores, editor; Alison Thiele, designer; Marcie Spence, photo researcher

Photo Credits
BigStockPhoto.com/Natures Lair, 20
Capstone Press/Karon Dubke, 4 (all), 6 (egg), 10, 18
Courtesy of Lisa Brown, 16
Dwight R. Kuhn, cover (egg and nymph), 8, 12
James P. Rowan, 14
Paula Stephens/123RF, cover (adult), 6
Shutterstock/Emily Sartoski, 1